THE
TIME MANAGEMENT
POCKETBOOK

Mike Clayton
Drawings by Phil Hailstone

057624

"A handy pocketbook guide packed with hints, tips and techniques that will help anyone who has ever struggled with 'getting it all done'. A pick 'n' mix of tools and ideas presented in Mike's engaging, easy-read style, this is one to have ready to hand in your desk, kitchen or workshop drawer."
Graeme Rees, Director, Trend Control Systems Ltd

"In business and life, time is precious – this wonderful book will make sure you make the most of it."
Paul Griffiths, Head of Operations, Mary Rose Trust

Published by:
Management Pocketbooks Ltd
Wild's Yard, The Dean, Alresford, Hants SO24 9BQ, U.K.
Tel: +44 (0)1962 735573 Fax: +44 (0)1962 733637
E-mail: sales@pocketbook.co.uk
Website: www.pocketbook.co.uk

KIDDERMINSTER COLLEGE
LEARNING RESOURCES CENTRE

Date:	16 03 18
Accession no:	057624
Classification:	658.4093 CLA

© Mike Clayton 2017

This edition published 2017
ISBN 978 1 910186 01 5
E-book ISBN 978 1 907078 73 6

British Library Cataloguing-in-Publication Data – A catalogue record for this book is available
from the British Library.

Design, typesetting and graphics by **zpek ltd**.   Printed in U.K.

CONTENTS

 TAKE CONTROL OF YOUR TIME 5
The basic process for using your time well, a simple & flexible plan, when to plan, what is your purpose?, what do you need to do to achieve your goals?, use your to do list properly, projects you don't have time for, how to allocate your tasks, understand your personal energy cycle, when to have meetings

 OVERCOME THE CHALLENGE OF TOO MUCH 47
Why is time management hard?, prioritising your work, which idea next?, the failure of multi-tasking, overload & overwhelm, how to delegate, negotiating more time, how to say NO, getting behind, handling your backlog – 4Rs, always on, sometimes off, social media & email, hanging on the telephone, distractions, preventing interruptions, beat procrastination

 BOOST YOUR PRODUCTIVITY 29
The power of the right routines, productive working routines, organisation & systems, the 5S approach to organisation, planning, preparation & follow-up, perfect preparation prevents poor performance, postparation, deadlines, milestones & self-motivation

 EVERYONE HAS A SYSTEM 81
Learn from the best, eating frogs, Italian tomatoes, getting things done, setting your focus, urgent & important, a chain of success, Kanban, software

 STRATEGIC TIME MANAGEMENT 99
Time is more valuable than any resource, executive busyness, initiative overload, investment in resources, leadership leverage, strategic responsibilities, time budget, organisational time, the gift of time, the nature of time

AUTHOR'S FOREWORD

There are no original ideas in Time Management; just original ways of expressing them. It is a privilege to be asked to create an all-new Time Management Pocketbook after five editions of such a worthy predecessor.

You won't find any disagreement from me with the ideas Ian Fleming put into his Time Management Pocketbook. What you will find is a different emphasis, and new ways of expressing the ideas, which I hope will resonate with you.

Many of the tools and models are my own. But I also want to acknowledge that much of the best thinking about how to help you manage your time has been done by a series of writers and trainers who each have their preferred method. Which one will work best for you, I cannot know.

So I have presented eight 'systems'. Where others have originated them, or made them their own in compelling descriptions, I can only say that if I misrepresent their ideas, the fault is mine alone, and solely due to my desire to encapsulate a big idea in a small space.

TAKE CONTROL
OF YOUR TIME

TAKE CONTROL OF YOUR TIME

YOU CANNOT MANAGE TIME...
BUT YOU CAN CONTROL HOW YOU USE IT

The ticking of a clock.
The passing of the days.
The rhythm of weeks.
The cycles of the moon.
...and another year is gone.

What makes you think you can manage any of that? You cannot.

Yet many of us feel we need to pack more and more into each day. We need to get more done, check more messages, engage with more people on social media, give more time to our families, and make more of our lives.

Productivity is our mantra, and getting stuff done is our goal. And to do it, we need to manage our time. But we cannot.

All we can do is learn how to use the time that we have, as well as we can.

TAKE CONTROL OF YOUR TIME

USE YOUR TIME AS WELL AS YOU CAN

This book is about how to use your time as well as you can. It's in five sections.

Section 1 will show you how to plan your time, to balance the advantages of feeling in control against the necessity of remaining flexible and able to adapt to changes.

Section 2 deals with ways of working that will make you more productive. View each idea as a tweak that will help you get more out of each day.

Section 3 tackles one of the biggest problems you face: the challenge of too much. Whether you have too much to do, too many messages and social media feeds, too many distractions, or a backlog of all of it, we have strategies to help you.

Section 4 will save you time. So you don't have to read a load of other books, we've summarised eight of the most popular time management systems out there, for you.

Section 5 introduces you to the idea of time as a strategic asset in your organisation. Without it, you'll achieve nothing, so what's the organisational perspective on time?

TAKE CONTROL OF YOUR TIME

THE BASIC PROCESS FOR USING YOUR TIME WELL

Planning your day, your week, or your month is a good thing.
But an hour into the morning, when the phone rings…

There goes your plan.

So you need two things:

1. A plan that is simple and adaptable.

2. An approach to reviewing your plan when you need to.

8

TAKE CONTROL OF YOUR TIME

A SIMPLE & FLEXIBLE PLAN

There are four components to a simple, flexible plan for how to use your time.

Goals
First – you need to know what you want to achieve: your goals.

Tasks
Second – your plan must list what you need to do to achieve your goals: your tasks.

Durations
Third – estimate how long each task will take: your durations.

Allocations
Fourth – decide what time slot to fit each task into: your allocations.

Goals – Tasks – Durations – Allocations... GTDA
You can remember this acronym as telling you how to *Get Things Done Adaptably*.

KEEP IT ADAPTABLE: REVIEW YOUR PLAN WHEN YOU NEED TO

Modern working life is full of interruptions. The phone rings, an email pings, or a colleague turns up at your desk. Your plan is out of date already.

So you need a process called *'meerkating'*.

Meerkats ferret around looking for food on the floor. But every now and then, the whole troupe will stand up on its hind legs and look around. They are scanning all the way out to the horizon, looking for anything.

And if they see anything that disturbs them… they change their plan.

You must be like a meerkat. Regularly survey everything that's going on. And, if you need to; change your plan.

WHEN TO PLAN

If you are new to regularly planning your time, start with creating a daily plan. The best time to do it is to make it the last thing you do at the end of each day. That way, when you start the next day, you already know what you are doing, and you can dive straight in.

Decide what goals you want to achieve tomorrow. Then list the tasks you need to do to achieve those goals. Estimate a duration for each task. And then allocate each task into your day. Leave spaces to catch up, or deal with things that emerge during the day.

As you get more practised, the best approach is often to plan a week ahead, before your new week starts. Use your diary or a one-page week planner, to put your tasks into your week. Leave enough gaps for the unexpected but inevitable things that will take over your diary.

TAKE CONTROL OF YOUR TIME

 ## UNDERSTAND WHAT YOU WANT TO ACHIEVE

Your **goals** are the things you want to achieve. They are the changes you want to make. So they should be the driving force of your plan.

Your goals matter... or they should. Selecting the right goals for tomorrow, or next week, is the start of prioritising how to use your time.

The way to find your goals is to ask yourself:

> What do I want to be different, this time tomorrow, or this time next week?

A good way to think about your planning goals is to think of them as worthwhile changes you want to bring about.

(12)

TAKE CONTROL OF YOUR TIME

 WHAT IS YOUR PURPOSE?

Good goals need to fit into a bigger picture.

Your work goals need be consistent with the purpose of your job. To set good goals, you need to know:

- What is your job description and what does your contract say?
- Whom do you serve and what value can you bring?
- What are your organisation's strategies, objectives, and priorities?
- What do your bosses and managers expect of you?

The same thing is true for other areas of your life, whether it is personal activities, your interests, family or social activities, or stuff you do in your community.

Know what matters to you and the people that you care about. Then set goals that will make worthwhile changes you want to create.

TAKE CONTROL OF YOUR TIME

 ## DON'T BE GREEDY

Too many people set themselves up to fail... day after day. They never achieve all their daily targets, and they end each day with a list of things they wanted to achieve, but haven't. And one reason for this series of failures stands out: they set too many goals for the day, the week, or the month.

Let's put aside the problem that too many goals means too little focus. Though important, **this is not the issue.**

When you plan your day, do you look at the day and think: *'Hmm... 8 hours. I'll plan 8 hours' worth of tasks.'?* That's tempting. But how many days do you get to use the full eight hours on the tasks you planned? Instead, think: *'Hmm... 8 hours. But I have 2 hours of meetings and I'm bound to spend 2 more dealing with interruptions and unexpected problems. I'll plan 4 hours' worth of tasks.'*

For you it may not be two hours of interruptions. It may be three, or four, or even six. Start your plan with only the amount of ambition that matches a **realistic** assessment of how much time you'll have. Don't be greedy, or you'll set yourself up to fail.

(14)

(T) WHAT DO YOU NEED TO DO TO ACHIEVE YOUR GOALS?

Now you know what your goals are for tomorrow, or next week.

Your next step is to make a list of the **tasks** you need to carry out, to achieve those goals.

Instinctive time-managers like lists
They get a buzz from ticking things off. Some even prefer to scrub things out. In fact, some people get a visceral satisfaction from crossing something off their list.

And that's good. Research by Teresa Amabile and Steven Kramer showed that people go home feeling better when they have a sense of having achieved things during their day at work. A list sets you up nicely for that.

15

YOUR TASK LIST IS NOT A TO DO LIST

The commonest approach to time management is the To Do list.

But this can be a toxic approach. You never seem to get to the end of it. The better you are at getting stuff done, the more things you keep adding to your To Do list. At the end of each day there's still a load of things to do. It's demotivating.

But your task list is not a list of things to do. It's a list of things you will do, to reach your goals. It is constrained, by careful selection, to which goals you are pursuing. And therefore, your list of tasks is fixed.

As you get stuff done, your task list reduces. At the end of the day, or the week, when your task list is finished, you've achieved your goals.

USE YOUR TO DO LIST PROPERLY

As you work through your task list, you may still be adding to your To Do list.

Used properly, your To Do list is not about managing your time. It's for managing your memory.

Use your To Do list to store ideas for things you could do. Whenever something crops up, add it to your list. That way, you don't have to remember it. Storing stuff like this in your memory uses up valuable mental resources. It gets in the way of focusing on what's important: today's tasks.

So, your To Do list is really a Could Do list
It's a list of things you could do, either to further one of your goals, or to kick-off a new goal. When it's time to make your new plan, you can use your Could Do list as a source of reminders and ideas for things that you could do.

- Which items represent a worthwhile change?
- Is now the right time to put them on your next plan?

STUFF THAT GETS STUCK ON YOUR LIST

Have you ever noticed things getting stuck on your To Do list? Weeks go by, and you don't get around to doing them, even though you think you should. If you had to do them, you would. That's to say, if there were real consequences to not doing them, rather than just feeling that you ought to do them.

And if you wanted to do them, you would. That's to say, if it would be a pleasure to do them, rather than just discharging a loose sense of obligation.

But actually, these are stuck in the middle, between 'must do' and 'want to do'. And all they give you is a sense of guilt. Guilt is not good, so do yourself a favour. Cross all these *'Should Do'* items off your list. If they ever become essential… you'll put them back.

'But hang on', you say. 'There's something there that is important. I just haven't started it, because I don't have the time…'

TAKE CONTROL OF YOUR TIME

 PROJECTS YOU DONT HAVE TIME FOR

There may be things on your To Do list that you just don't have time to get to.

But these aren't To Do items at all. A To Do item is a task that won't take very long. If it were important, you'd do it. These things are too big for that. They'd take too long, because there are really a whole load of tasks in there. And maybe a whole goal.

These aren't To Do items; they are projects
The way to test a project is to take the To Do item, and write it as a title at the top of a new page in your notebook. This is your project.

Next, list the first three tasks that you need to do, to kick-off your project. Make these as small, as quick, and as easy as possible. Put them in your diary, so they get done.

If you do all three tasks, you'll know whether you want to continue, and plan this project out fully, or if it's not important enough, yet. If that's the case, look forward to the section on *'The challenge of too much'* (see page 47).

(19)

TAKE CONTROL OF YOUR TIME

 ESTIMATE HOW LONG EACH TASK WILL TAKE

The trickiest of the four steps is estimating how long each task will take you. That's because people are pretty poor at estimating.

So why bother?
That's a good question. In one branch of project management, there is a whole movement called #NoEstimates. But without estimating durations, you can't know:

- Whether your plan is realistic for the whole day or whole week

- Where each task can fit, between existing commitments in your day

- How you are doing, as you progress through your day

- What the implications are, when things take longer than you expected

(20) So estimating the duration for each task is important.

D **TIPS FOR ESTIMATING**

Because estimating is tricky, here is a list of six tips and tricks to help you.

Tip 1 Have you done something like this before? If you have, how did it work out? What snags did you encounter? What went well? How long did it take?

Tip 2 Can you break the task down into steps or smaller tasks? If you can, estimate the duration of each of these individually, then add a bit of time for the transitions between them.

Tip 3 Have you allowed time to get ready for the task, time for breaks, time to review and improve your work, and time to tidy up afterwards?

Tip 4 We all under-estimate how long it takes us to do things. But we tend to be more realistic about our friends or colleagues. Clearly, they don't have the superpowers we do! So don't estimate how long it will take you… Estimate how long the same task would take your friend or your colleague.

TIPS FOR ESTIMATING

Tip 5 Things always take longer than we expect. So add some extra time, just in case. This will accommodate snags, setbacks, and snafus.

Tip 6 Does this task involve other people? If it does, then allow extra time for explaining, for complexity, for waiting, and for their mistakes. More people mean more extra time. Often, if you double the number of people, you need to quadruple the extra time. If the extra time for one person is M minutes, the extra time for 2 people is 4xM, for 3 people it's 9xM and for 4 people it's 16xM.

Get good at estimating
The more estimating you do, the better you will get at it. This doesn't mean you'll always get it right. After all, stuff happens. And new tasks that you've never done before will always be a challenge. But if you estimate a lot, you'll start to find that many of your estimates are pretty good. And some will be uncannily precise.

TAKE CONTROL OF YOUR TIME

DECIDE WHAT TIME SLOT TO FIT EACH TASK INTO

Of the four steps in your time planning process, **allocation** could be the most important. It's the one that will give you a real sense of control over how you use your time.

It's also the easiest to do. It needs no original thinking or working stuff out. You just allocate each task into a slot in your diary. As long as it fits, you're fine.

But despite this being important and easy, this is where most people stop. They don't do this, so they get caught with interruptions:

- *'Have you got a moment?'*

- *'Could you just... ?'*

So now, since there's nothing committed into your schedule for the day, you say, *'Yes, what is it?'* And there goes your time; trickling away.

The alternative is to say, *'How important is it? I have something scheduled for now.'*

(23)

TAKE CONTROL OF YOUR TIME

 ## HOW TO ALLOCATE YOUR TASKS

Too often, you get to the end of the day and you've been busy all day. But it feels like you've not got much done. And, crucially, you still have one or two big things left over.

Chances are, you've broken the law...
We're talking about Parkinson's Law, here. Back in the 1950s, Cyril Northcote Parkinson discovered that *'work expands to fill the time available'*. His finding has now been promoted to the status of 'law' and named after him.

And it's very much true, in a world of email and Facebook. You know that if you haven't got much on, then you can fill your whole morning with that kind of trivia. But if you're busy with something that matters, you can usually fit in a short slot to clear all your important messages in 15 minutes before lunch.

So, **allocation Rule No.1:** Allocate the big things into your day or your week first. Fit the small things around them.

TAKE CONTROL OF YOUR TIME

 WHERE TO PUT EACH TASK

When are you at your best?

- Is it first thing?
- Or maybe it's around coffee time?
- Perhaps it's after lunch?
- Or maybe late afternoon?

Whichever it is, the best time to allocate for your biggest, most complex, most demanding task… is then.

Maybe you have another good slot where you can allocate another important task.

And what about those sluggish times, when you're at your worst? Use those to allocate the small, simple, low-priority tasks that won't need much concentration.

So, **allocation Rule No.2:** Allocate the big things into your best times of day. Fit the little things into your dips.

(25)

TAKE CONTROL OF YOUR TIME

 UNDERSTAND YOUR PERSONAL ENERGY CYCLE

These peaks and troughs in your day create your own personal energy cycle. What does yours look like?

Think of your tasks as grapes, apples, and pineapples. Allocate the biggest to the times when you're at your best, and the grapes to the dips.

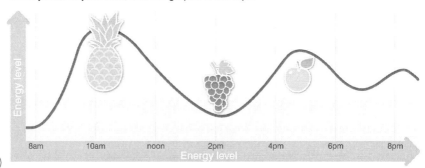

TAKE CONTROL OF YOUR TIME

BOOSTING YOUR ENERGY

How can you raise the peaks and smooth out the dips in your energy? Here are some top tips:

- Take breaks – working too long is poor for concentration and posture
- Keep hydrated – have a glass of water near at hand, if you can
- Limit use of caffeine – if you do, then tea and coffee will give you a boost
- Healthy snacks – sugar gives a quick boost but then a crash
- Get up and move around – better still, get outside for fresh air and natural light
- Are you allowed naps where you work? If so, these can give you a big re-charge
- Novelty can boost concentration – if you're getting bored, swap tasks

So, **allocation Rule No.3:** Manage your energy levels to get more done.

WHEN TO HAVE MEETINGS

You may not be in control of this. Your meeting times may be allocated by other people. If so, move along... nothing for you here.

But if you do have a say in when to schedule your meetings, what is best?
If you are an extravert and find being with people energises you, the best times to allocate to meetings are when your energy dips. That way, you get a free boost.

If you are an introvert, and you find being with people takes energy and concentration, the best times to allocate to meetings are when your energy levels are high. Otherwise you'll find yourself struggling to contribute well.

So, **allocation Rule No.4:** If you can, arrange meetings to fit your introvert/extravert personality trait.

BOOST YOUR PRODUCTIVITY

WE ALL WANT MORE

We all want more. We want to do more, achieve more, and get more. And for that, the silver bullet is productivity.

Productivity: *the ability to make, do, and create things, abundantly and efficiently.*

That sounds good… let's get started.

Not so fast
Have you heard the phrase *'more haste: less speed'*? Sometimes you have to go slowly to build up speed, and productivity is definitely an example.

A lot of the guidance you'll get here is very much in this vein; but if you follow these tips you will find you are soon able to get more done. And if you are setting the right goals, you'll become highly effective in what you choose to do.

BOOST YOUR PRODUCTIVITY

THE POWER OF THE RIGHT ROUTINES

We all have our own routines. They simplify our lives and are often comforting; especially in times of change or when you're under pressure.

But the power of routine goes beyond making your life easy and comfortable. If you choose the right routines they can do two very important things that will boost your productivity:

1. They can set you up so that you can focus on what matters, because you've taken care of the infrastructure around doing it.

2. They relieve you of a lot of choices. Each choice needs a decision and each decision takes effort. As a result, you are left with diminished resources for other, more important decisions.

We'll look at four types of routine that can help you 'automate' how you handle your wellbeing, the start of your working day, your work cycle and the gaps.

BOOST YOUR PRODUCTIVITY

ROUTINES FOR YOUR WELLBEING

Three things go together in a tightly bound triad: physical wellbeing, mental wellbeing, and productive capacity. Notice, by the way, the word 'capacity'. You do need to exert willpower to actually be productive!

Looking after your mind and body comes down to four things.

Fuel: Good quality food is vital for both physical and mental health.

Exercise: Build some form of routine exercise into your life.

Rest: Create a sound night-time routine and prioritise sufficient good quality sleep.

Relationships: The quality of your relationships has a huge impact on your mental and emotional wellness.

This is not the Pocketbook to tell you how to get these right. But if you build strong routines around each (and they often go well together), your productivity will increase.

BOOST YOUR PRODUCTIVITY

CRAFT YOUR MORNING ROUTINE

Mornings are where your day starts, so it's the key place to find a routine that works for you. Because everyone is different, it would be wrong to prescribe a routine, just because it works for one person or another.

However, you can be sure of some of the ingredients of a good morning routine.

Wakefulness
We are often at our most creative when we have just woken up. But we are rarely at our most rational, so depending on what you need to do, choose whether to start with a wake-up routine, or to go straight into creative work.

Hydration
We lose fluids while we sleep, and your brain can't function at full capacity when even slightly dehydrated. So drink some water.

Self-care
There are more than good social reasons for preparing yourself for the day. Your transition to being fresh, clean, groomed, and dressed can trigger a change in mood.

BOOST YOUR PRODUCTIVITY

PRODUCTIVE WORKING ROUTINES

Finding a productive working routine can be a big challenge for many people. Modern working life seems to have evolved to counter good practices.

It creates interruptions and distractions, and often discourages good breaks. Meetings can be back-to-back with no time to get from one to the next, let alone reflect on what you've heard, process the ideas, and act on your commitments.

We'll talk about preparation later in this section, and distractions in the next. Suffice to say: minimising distractions, maximising good preparation, and taking proper regular breaks are all routines that will boost your productivity.

Hydration… again
If your workplace permits it, keep water close at hand. Your brain will dehydrate and drop in performance before you think to get a drink. But, if there's one to hand, you'll automatically take sips and stay close to optimum hydration. And that means peak productivity.

PRODUCTIVE WORKING ROUTINES

Environment
Environment is important. Many workplaces offer constraints, but adapt your environment as best you can to what works well for you: spartan and clear, or cluttered and homely; bright and vibrant, or cosy and muted; and music or noise, or silence.

Email and messages
If you are working with a computer, only have open the apps you are actively working with. Close others down. The time cost is countered by the reduced distraction.

In particular, when you aren't actively using them, close down your email and messaging applications. This is specially so when you are working on big, important tasks. Many of us are at our best at the start of the day. And emails often represent the grapes we referred to (see page 26) when thinking of energy cycles. As a result, aim to do your first task before you open your email program and check your messages.

PRODUCTIVE USE OF GAPS

We all have gaps in our days. Sometimes too few. But if you want to be productive, you need to use them well.

The first thing to note is that using a gap well does not necessarily mean *'doing something'*. Actively choosing to rest or recharge is a positive and productive use. But you may choose to do something to make the most of your time. Arriving at a meeting early, waiting for a train, the spaces between events. Even your commute.

The secret is to have things with you that you can do, like reading, an audio book, or paperwork, for example. Modern phones and tablets mean you can have a vast resource of archived reading, part-finished documents, learning materials, and planning tools ready to hand at all times.

And here's the kicker. That 15-minute gap can be a hugely productive time. It's sandwiched between a specific activity at each end and, because it's a bonus, there is no anxiety about the need to do something, so you are free to focus 100 percent.

ORGANISATION & SYSTEMS

To many people, organisation and systems sound dull. And there is certainly an investment to setting them up at the outset.

But the investment can be very minor if you do it right
Rather than attempt to create a Grand System, instead create incremental improvements. If your filing isn't working, adopt a new process; but don't re-file everything. Instead, put every file you use into the new system. After a while, the files left in the old system will be those you use so rarely, that you can safely archive them.

We mentioned a conducive working environment earlier (see page 35). For many people (but maybe not you) this means tidy. For most people, tidy means less distraction and easier retrieval of the things you need. You can focus on finding solutions rather than finding stationery.

BOOST YOUR PRODUCTIVITY

THE 5S APPROACH TO ORGANISATION

The Japanese 5S system takes its name from five processes all starting with the S sound in Japanese. Thankfully, the flexibility of the English language allows us to keep the 5S formulation with a near enough perfect match in meanings.

Sort (Seiri)
Put the things you use most often, nearest to you. Put everything else further away.

Systematise (Seiton)
Everything should have a place where it belongs, so you can find it easily.

Sweep (Seito)
Keep your workplace clean, tidy, and clutter free.

Standardise (Seiketsu)
Standardise the processes and procedures you use (we'll talk about checklists next).

Sustain (Shitsuke)
Make your good practices into habit; including the habit of constant improvement.

BOOST YOUR PRODUCTIVITY

CHECKLISTS SAVE LIVES

They use them in hospitals; in accident and emergency and in theatre. They use them in the military, they use them in heavy engineering and manufacturing, and they use them in the cockpits of commercial airliners. Checklists save lives.

☐ **Checklists also save time**
No thinking what to do next or figuring out how to get the job done.

☐ **Checklists avoid pointless repetition**
Do the task, check it off. Hence the name.

☐ **Checklists prevent mistakes and missed steps**
You've checked it off, now do the next thing.

☐ **Checklists reduce stress**
No job seems as daunting when it is broken down into lots of little tasks.

Create your own checklists to guide you through important repeated tasks.

BOOST YOUR PRODUCTIVITY

ORGANISED FILING vs MESSY CHAOS

In his book, *'Messy'*, Tim Harford argues for a move away from traditional filing.

The benefits of filing are familiar – you can access what you need, when you need it, quickly and easily. And in the days of paper files, if it wasn't filed, your only recourse was to go through every document until you found it.

But filing systems can fail. And with ever increasing volumes of data, they take even more time to create, while a rigid system can expend effort into filing away stuff you'll never need again.

Electronic filing has been supplemented by ever-improved electronic search. Save time by not filing, and let the search tool take the strain. The challenge here, though, is which of 20 or 2,000 or 20 million results is the one you need?

The balance is a simple filing system. Use a small number of broad categories to put important documents into piles. Now you know where to target your search. Spend time finding the right balance for you. When I was a student, my professor, Henry Hall, referred to the mess in his office as a *'piling system'*. He was years ahead of his time!

BOOST YOUR PRODUCTIVITY

PLANNING, PREPARATION & FOLLOW-UP

Jump straight to task, and then move on when it is done. This sounds like a prescription for efficiency, but it is certainly not a route to effectiveness. And being productive at the price of doing the wrong things is a false bargain. Effective productivity means three habits:

Planning
Creating a plan that, at its simplest, is your Goal, Tasks, Durations, and Allocations. If your work involves other people or needs materials or equipment, you'll need to do more. You may also need to anticipate problems and setbacks, and plan for risks.

Preparation
Never go into any situation without taking time to prepare yourself. That's how meetings become a waste of time, and presentations crash and burn.

Follow-up
If it's worth doing, it's worth reflecting on, reviewing, and honouring any commitments you made as part of the process. Documenting, tidying up, and yes, filing.

BOOST YOUR PRODUCTIVITY

THE SIMPLE SECRET OF PLANNING

Step 1: Where are we going?
Set a destination: your goal
and objectives.

Step 2: How do we get there?
The tasks involved, how long they will take,
and when each will be done.

Step 3: What resources do we need?
People, materials, equipment, assets and, putting them
all together: budget.

Step 4: What could go wrong?
If you can foresee problems, you can minimise their likelihood of
occurring or their impact. Or you can come up with a Plan B.

Step 5: How can we measure progress?
Find a small number of measurable factors that you can track, to give you a clear
indication of whether you are on plan, or have slipped and need to make changes.

42

PERFECT PREPARATION PREVENTS POOR PERFORMANCE

We've had 5S; here's 5P.

One of the problems with back-to-back meetings is the lack of time it gives you to prepare. Have you ever seen people in meetings who just look shell-shocked for the first 15 minutes?

The people who get the best results at meetings prepare in advance and then make sure they have a few minutes to gather their thoughts and remind themselves of their priorities, just before the meeting starts.

Back-to-back meetings? If you have any say in the matter, schedule yours for 25, 50, or 75 minutes, instead of 30, 60, or 90.

And what about presenters who hardly seem to know what's on their slides? You wouldn't expect an actor to come on stage as Hedda or Hamlet, without having rehearsed. It's their job. So why do so many business people treat presentations as a chance to show their improvisation skills?

BOOST YOUR PRODUCTIVITY

POSTPARATION: A NEW WORD FOR FOLLOW-UP

If you can prepare, why can't you postpare? And if your meeting, presentation, or event is important enough to prepare for, then it's also important enough to postpare from.

Research on wisdom and learning shows that people who deliberately reflect on their experiences learn better than their peers who don't. They make better judgements and become more widely respected. Indeed, decision-makers who analyse the outcomes of their choices – successful and not – become better decision-makers.

So, make it a habit to tidy up after yourself physically and mentally. Do the work you committed to do, send your thank you messages, and mentally review what happened, and what could have happened differently. Actors get notes from their director before and after their performances. Be your own director.

44

BOOST YOUR PRODUCTIVITY

DEADLINES & SELF-MOTIVATION

Deadlines motivate most of us to perform on time. As the deadline looms, urgency kicks in and productivity takes off.

Deadlines are a great motivator. But recognise that they motivate by fear. For some people, too many deadlines create unsupportable levels of stress. And too much stress harms productivity. Or, equally likely, you'll trade productivity for quality.

But deadlines are a great way to deal with one of those insidious productivity thieves: procrastination. If you find yourself prone to putting things off, one solution is to set a deadline. And since deadlines imply consequences*, you need to attach a consequence.

An easy consequence to set is embarrassment; losing face. Tell people when you'll complete your task and let them hold you to account.

The original deadline was a line outside the Andersonville prisoner of war camp in the American Civil War. Anyone crossing it would be shot. That's a consequence!

MILESTONES & SELF-MOTIVATION

Milestones are like deadlines. But the mood music is different. Milestones are positive. When we reach them, we've achieved something worthwhile.

The more milestones you set yourself, the more visible your progress will be. This will create a sense of achievement and a reason to celebrate.

When you celebrate your successes, you notice them and become more confident. This can lead to more enthusiasm and better performance. In turn, these create more success and the achievement of more milestones.

If you celebrate those, you complete the loop. It's a positive cycle that can drive your productivity onwards and upwards.

MILESTONE 10

OVERCOME THE CHALLENGE OF TOO MUCH

WHY IS TIME MANAGEMENT HARD?

The biggest challenge of time management is not planning how to use your time. And neither is it in getting stuff done productively. Rather, it is coping with the vast number of things you could be doing.

This requires four principal skills:

 Deciding what is important.

 Focusing on what is important.

 Managing the excess of calls on your time.

 Putting aside the things that aren't important.

In this section, we'll examine the tools you need for each of these skills.

PRIORITISING YOUR WORK

Deciding what is most important can be bewildering when you have too much choice.

In *'The Paradox of Choice'*, Barry Schwartz describes how too many options make deciding difficult. We worry about what we'd be putting aside and missing out on. However, a large part of your success won't come from what you do, but from what you choose to put aside. If you try to do everything, you're unlikely to do anything well.

Putting aside the trivial is hard enough. But what about when you have to put aside something valuable, to make space for something else, that is still more valuable?

The key concept is **'importance'**. Do the work that is important. How will you know **what** is important? You can only define it in terms of your goals. If doing something will help you achieve what you most want; then it is important. At work, if something supports the purpose of your job; it's important.

Of course not everyone has (or feels they have) choice. That can lead to feelings of overwhelm, or to genuine overload. We'll tackle those later.

OVERCOME THE CHALLENGE OF TOO MUCH

THE CHOICE TO FOCUS

Vilfredo Pareto was an Italian economist. In 1896, he discovered that 80 percent of Italy's wealth belonged to 20 percent of its citizens. This 80/20 power law now bears his name – thanks to management consultant Joseph Juran.

Pareto's law suggests that most of the value of many groups lies in a small number of the highest value members. That's how nature works. Most of the world's river water flows through a few great rivers, and most of its population lives in the few largest nations.

Likewise, most of the value your work can deliver will come from working on the few most valuable things.

This doesn't just apply to trivia. Some pretty important things still have far less impact than other things you could choose to do. You will be successful to the extent you are able to choose wisely where to put your focus.

The difficulty is figuring out which things to focus on. I call this the *'Pareto Problem'.*

THE CHOICE TO FOCUS

At the bottom left of the Pareto Chart, if you do one thing, it makes a big contribution to your work or your life. Near the top right, however, each new thing you do makes a marginal improvement at best. You have to do a lot, to get a little.

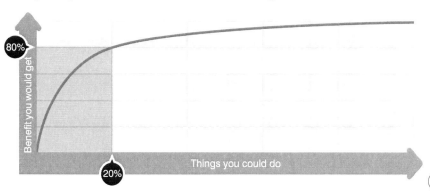

80%

Benefit you would get

Things you could do

20%

51

OVERCOME THE CHALLENGE OF TOO MUCH

TOO MANY IDEAS

A really good example of the Pareto Problem is that long list of good ideas that accumulates on your To Do List.

I'm not talking about all the trivia; but the big things. In the first section (see page 19) we suggested that you turn these into projects. But what if you are one of those people who has loads of ideas for projects? And they are all good ideas… or could be.

Get yourself a notebook – it could be an app on your phone, tablet, or computer. Mine is a traditional paper notebook. Use it to document all your project ideas. For each new idea, start a page and make notes and drawings to ensure you won't forget.

This gets the idea out of your brain, where it can worm a hole in your concentration. It means you won't worry about forgetting it. It also allows you to evaluate the idea against others, when you know you have time for a new project.

You will be more objective in your assessment after time has passed, and you can focus today on the projects you have already committed to.

WHICH IDEA NEXT?

You have a dozen projects you could take on next. There are plenty that seem appealing. So, what do you do when it's time to choose what to start on? With so many things in your head, or in your project list, how do you sort them? The answer comes back to your goals, or what you see as your purpose.

In whatever way suits you best, do a brain dump and get all your ideas in front of you. Then sort them into a small number of categories. These might include:

- Things I thought were a good idea, but I don't now

- Things I'd love to pursue, but won't be worth it

- Things I feel I ought to pursue, but I'd hate it

- Things that will make a real difference to what matters to me

Take your time. Use different criteria to evaluate your choices. Sleep on your best options for a few nights. Talk to people whose opinions you trust. And, in the end, accept that the second or third best idea executed with commitment, focus, and vigour will always outperform the best idea implemented half-heartedly.

OVERCOME THE CHALLENGE OF TOO MUCH

THE FAILURE OF MULTI-TASKING

Let's get straight to the point: multi-tasking is a poor choice at best, and a disastrous one at worst. Yes, you can walk and talk at the same time. But as soon as you try to do two mentally demanding tasks at once, your brain will overload. What we think of as multi-tasking is really *'serial mono-tasking'*. That is, you do one thing for a short while, switch attention and do another, then switch back.

The switching of attention is inefficient. Do it too often, and you will waste a lot of time as the little cut-over times add up. And you can easily confuse yourself, letting information from one task contaminate your assessments in the other.

If you don't switch often enough, your working memory will lose track of the detail of the task you're switching to, and you'll use up time recalling where you'd got to. Put simply, **don't do it**. Instead, allocate chunks of time to work on one thing. Make substantial progress and stop at a natural break point.

OVERCOME THE CHALLENGE OF TOO MUCH

BUT I MUST MULTI-TASK...

You may be one of those people who says *'I have so much on, I just have to multi-task.'* Well, if that is true, here are some tips. The first one is **'don't'**, but if you must:

1. Blocks of around 20 minutes optimise the balance between too many short bursts, and losing track of where you were.

2. You'll respond best to the mental and physical demands if you prioritise rest, and take good breaks.

3. Keep your multi-tasking to simpler things, and ideally swap between different categories of activity to avoid *'mental contamination'*.

4. Younger adults seem to cope best with multi-tasking. And yes, there is experimental evidence that women are marginally less rubbish at multi-tasking on certain types of (low-demand) tasks.

OVERCOME THE CHALLENGE OF TOO MUCH

OVERLOAD & OVERWHELM

These are two words that are very familiar to many people in their working lives. The first thing we must do is distinguish between them.

Overload is an **objective** state. It is when you have so much to do, that you **cannot expect to complete it all,** in the time allowed, with the resources you have available to you.

Overwhelm is a **subjective** state. It is when you **feel that you cannot cope** with the amount that you have to do, in the time allowed, with the resources you have available to you.

The challenge of overload is how best to use your time to make the most effective progress; for the greatest benefit to yourself, your employer, or your community.

Overwhelm is a stress response. The challenge is to cope under pressure and regain your ability to focus on what matters.

OVERCOME THE CHALLENGE OF TOO MUCH

OVERCOMING OVERWHELM

Because overwhelm is a stress response, the solution is not better time management. Stress arises from a feeling that you aren't in control. In this case, overwhelm occurs when you don't feel in control of your workload.

So the solution is to take control.

1 The first step is to empty your head. Write a big list of everything that you feel you need to do. This is your *'Overwhelm List'*.

2 Then be ruthless and cross out the trivia. This is anything you really do not need to do.

3 Now look for things that can wait. Anything you can put off for a day or more, transfer onto a *'Tomorrow List'*. Then take it off your Overwhelm List.

What's left is today's challenge. If you're still feeling overwhelmed, don't worry. We're going to break a couple of time management rules to fix it. Because your problem isn't time management; it's stress.

OVERCOMING OVERWHELM

To continue:

4 Now highlight every small task on your list that you could do in five minutes or less. These are your *'Tiny Tasks'*.

5 Starting at the top of your list, do each of your Tiny Tasks as quickly as possible, and keep going for 20 minutes. Then stop, cross them off, and take a break.

6 In your break, pick one substantial task that you most want to work on (not necessarily the most important or most urgent – when you're stressed, motivation matters more).

7 After your break, spend 40 to 60 minutes completing that task, or making substantial progress, to a point where you can stop conveniently.

8 Take a longer break, and go back to step 5. Repeat the cycle, until you have no more Tiny Tasks. Now, your Overwhelm List is small, and you've made progress on some big tasks. You'll almost certainly be feeling back in control.

OVERCOME THE CHALLENGE OF TOO MUCH

DEALING WITH OVERLOAD

To deal with overload, we need to recall that overload is when you have so much to do that you cannot expect to complete it all, in the time allowed, with the resources you have available to you.

Therefore, there are three strategies to deal with overload:

1. **Increase the resources you have available**
   Either delegate to additional people, or spend money on ready-made solutions.

2. **Increase the amount of time available**
   Negotiate extensions to your deadlines.

3. **Reduce the amount of work to do**
   Either reduce the quantity or quality of your work.

HOW TO DELEGATE

Delegation is a way of increasing your resource base, so choose a process that will grow your capacity in the long term as well as fixing a problem now.

Match the right person for the task
Take account of people's abilities, aspirations, and existing commitments. Avoid favouritism, or using unwanted tasks as a penalty.

Brief the person well
If you leave gaps in your briefing, they will not be as self-sufficient as you intend, leaving you with more work than you'd hoped.

Tell them the context, what success will look like, how much autonomy you are giving them, and when you need them to complete the job. You may also need to spell out how to do the job, how you want them to keep you informed, and what equipment, materials, or help they can use.

HOW TO DELEGATE

Secure commitment
When you delegate, always ask three questions:

1. Do you understand what I want you to do?

2. Are you able to do what I want you to do?

3. Do you commit to do what I want you to do?

Monitor, guide and support
This is how you deal with the risk of delegating to someone else, and help your colleague to learn as they work.

Give recognition, praise, and feedback
When they complete the task, recognition, praise, and feedback will motivate them and help them to develop their skills and expertise.

OVERCOME THE CHALLENGE OF TOO MUCH

NEGOTIATING MORE TIME

When you want to negotiate more time (or, indeed, revised quality standards), remember that a compelling argument must have three components.

You
The person you're negotiating with must have reason to trust you. If you always deliver and have clearly assessed the situation fairly, your argument will have more sway than if you let people down, and are asking for more time for the wrong reason.

Your case
You must present a strong reason for the change you want. Show you have thought about the consequences and can answer the objections. Your reasoning must be sound, based on a fair assessment of the relevant facts.

Them
The person you want to persuade will base their judgement partly on the facts, and largely on how they feel. Anticipate their priorities and show how your proposal meets them and maybe even gives more of what they want.

OVERCOME THE CHALLENGE OF TOO MUCH

DOING LESS

The ultimate solution to overload is to do less. And that means saying 'no' to yourself and to others.

But we know that saying no is hard. It feels negative, people don't like it, and it removes the chance to do something and succeed.

Sadly though, as you progress through your career, there will be ever more things you could do, and saying yes to all of them will become increasingly hard to sustain. Indeed, people won't respect you if you say yes to everything: they'll just see you as a bit of an 'easy touch'.

The right strategy is to be prepared to say no to the right things. These are things that do not contribute enough. If you were to do them, then they would limit your ability to focus on things that matter more.

When you say no for the right reasons, and in a courteous and respectful way, this is not negative at all. Rather, it is a Noble Objection.

HOW TO SAY NO

So how do you make a **N**oble **O**bjection and say NO?

Evaluate your choice
If you are not certain whether something is right for a yes or a NO, find out more. Ask questions and test the possible outcomes to see which is right.

Clear, calm, confident, courteous
This is how to say NO. You may feel a need to apologise. That's fine, but express regret for the impact it has on the other person, not for your need to choose.

Never a naked NO
Always clothe your NO in a *'because'*. People accept a NO more easily when they know there is a good reason. And if your reasoning is flawed, it gives them a chance to ask you to reconsider.

Additionally, where you can, make helpful suggestions. These will show you are thoughtful and that you want to mitigate the impact of your NO.

64

OVERCOME THE CHALLENGE OF TOO MUCH

GETTING BEHIND

We all get behind from time to time. This creates a backlog of stuff you need to do. It may be a pile of papers to read, or bills to pay, or forms to complete. Perhaps it's an email inbox full of unanswered (or unread) emails. Or it might be a list of jobs around the house.

Whatever is in your backlog, it always has the same effect...

Backlogs bring us down. They sap us of our energy. We just look at them and feel guilt, obligation, duty. In this position, you can easily start to feel overwhelmed, so you move on. You ignore your backlog, so what happens? It just keeps growing.

Before you know it, it isn't a pile of stuff. It's a mountain. It's the Everest of task lists, and you are a *'bad person'* for letting it get that way.

But you don't have a route map, you don't have Sherpas, and you don't have the energy to tackle it. So the tectonic plates of your life just keep driving the mountain ever upwards.

OVERCOME THE CHALLENGE OF TOO MUCH

HANDLING YOUR BACKLOG – 4Rs

Remove

The first thing you need to do is remove your backlog to a place where it won't grab your attention and make you feel bad. Put your pile of papers in a file and put that on a shelf. Create an email folder called 'Backlog' and drop everything from your inbox into it. Take your list of household jobs off the counter and put it in a drawer.

With your backlog out of sight, you can deploy all your energy on your frontlog; the things that are current in your life.

But there's one thing you must do first…

Review

What if there is something in the backlog you removed that is important and urgent? Before you move on, look through your backlog for anything that should be in your frontlog. This quick, simple task can prevent you from misplacing something and missing a vital deadline.

OVERCOME THE CHALLENGE OF TOO MUCH

HANDLING YOUR BACKLOG – 4Rs

Reinvent

With your backlog out of the way, you can focus on your frontlog. But how did the backlog arise in the first place? Was it a peak in workload? If so, don't worry. You'll clear it in the next trough, and all will be well.

Or are you struggling to cope with your workload? That's more serious. In this case, you need to reinvent the way you handle your work. You need a new process, to be more productive, or a better way to reduce your workload through delegation, saying NO, or negotiating more sustainable standards.

Once you are on top of your current workload, you can…

Reduce

The last step is to tackle your backlog. Carve out a small amount of time on a regular basis – ideally daily, but weekly is fine. Use that time to deal with one or two items from the top of your backlog. It will diminish faster and faster, because as you move through it, the older things will increasingly not need you to do anything.

OVERCOME THE CHALLENGE OF TOO MUCH

ALWAYS ON

Work-life balance has been a 'big thing' in Western countries, since the 1980s. But we must remember that the term does not imply where the point of balance is or should be.

Your mental image may be 50:50, but that isn't necessarily right. It may be right for you, but is it right for me? And anyway, 50 percent of what? Does it mean 12 hours a day, or half your waking hours? Does it include weekends? And do you work in a one-day weekend or two-day weekend culture?

Work-life balance was always hard, but now many of us find our work follows us home in our pockets, and starts making little pinging noises and vibrating whenever the customer or the boss decides they require attention. And even if you don't need to deal with that, what about a constant stream of friend requests, social media updates, text messages, emails, image shares...?

How can you manage your time, in an *'always on'* culture where machines give everyone the ability to grab your attention at any time?

OVERCOME THE CHALLENGE OF TOO MUCH

SOMETIMES OFF

'Machines give everyone the ability to grab your attention…' but not the right to do so.

What if there were a way to stop this? What if you could deny the machine the ability to interrupt you constantly, so you can focus on what you choose to focus on?

What if it were simple to use? Just a simple thing you could do to deny access, and then undo to re-enable access when it suited you?

That technology is available. Or, maybe I should say 'is *still* available.' It's called an on-off switch, and all your devices have one.

You can turn off your phone, set your tablet to *'do not disturb'* and close the app on your computer. As I write this pocketbook, my browser is closed, my email client unopened, and I have alerts set to off. My phone is on silent, and my tablet is in another room. The secret is discipline.

OVERCOME THE CHALLENGE OF TOO MUCH

TAMING SOCIAL MEDIA

Human beings are social creatures and social interaction gives us a buzz. That's why social media can be almost addictive. Discipline really is your only choice.

So the key is to create habits that make discipline easier.

Since social media rarely require a lot of concentration, the best times to use them are when you cannot give your time to more substantial tasks. Short public transport journeys, waiting in queues, when you are tired, and on breaks, are good times to check and respond to your messages.

Perhaps the most important habit is to turn off the alerts that allow social media to grab your attention. That way, you will look at it only when **you** choose.

Another valuable habit is a periodic review of the people from whom you allow contact, the lists you subscribe to, and the groups to which you belong. Some sap energy and waste time. You joined a list last year, but now you aren't that interested… Unsubscribe.

OVERCOME THE CHALLENGE OF TOO MUCH

WRANGLING YOUR EMAIL

The number of emails we received was once a matter of pride. Now we get satisfaction from clearing them all down and achieving the nirvana of *'inbox zero'*.

Until… ping! In comes the next one.

Rule 1
As with social media, Rule 1 is to turn off the alerts. Better still, only open your email service when you plan to use it. Schedule your email activity and, better still, put a time box around it. The best times are between bigger, more substantial chunks of work.

Beware, a lot of the problems are caused by… you
Sending an email when you could make a phone call, and copying people into an email, who don't need to see it, are both habits that create email. So too is subscribing to newsletters. Periodically unsubscribe to newsletters you don't read.

(71)

OVERCOME THE CHALLENGE OF TOO MUCH

WRANGLING YOUR EMAIL

Use email wisely
It's not just whether you send, or who you send to; it's what you send. Make your email messages short and courteous. End them with a clear question, so the reply is as focused as your message. And be brief with your replies. Create a subject line that makes the content clear. In a big organisation, start habits you'd like others to pick up. In a small organisation, discuss and agree habits that will help everyone.

Now or then?
There's an old system that dates to paper memos: the one touch system. Look at everything once. Only check your messages when you have time to act on them so you don't waste time reading anything a second time. An alternative is this: if you can clear your email in under 5 minutes, do so now. If not, allocate a time to deal with it (which could be now, if it's urgent).

OVERCOME THE CHALLENGE OF TOO MUCH

WRANGLING YOUR EMAIL

Use the software's abilities to help you
Most email software has the ability to set up folders, rules, categories or tags, and priorities that will help you sort your incoming email. Here are some ideas for systems. Each works for some people, so combine the ones you think will help you.

- Create rules to file certain emails into specific folders

- Tag emails in your inbox with the day of the week you plan to action them

- Label emails as: for record, for reading, for action, or waiting for someone else, so you don't forget an outstanding action

- Set up the fields your inbox displays, which it sorts by, and which it groups by. For example, group by category, and sort within categories by date received

- Archive anything in your inbox older than 14 days

- Print long emails to read when travelling

OVERCOME THE CHALLENGE OF TOO MUCH

WRANGLING YOUR EMAIL

Beware of errors
Automation has its perils. Occasionally a rule applied correctly gives the wrong result. Especially when your software's automatic routines put your boss's email in your junk folder. So periodically scan your automated folders.

Conflict is the biggest time waster
So avoid it. Re-read every message for unintended discourtesy – especially if you choose to be blunt or need to disagree. Sometimes, it pays to put it aside for 24 hours, or ask a colleague to read it. Unreasonable deadlines also cause conflict. You waste your time chasing progress, and they get upset or angry. Remember, email is not an instant message tool.

OVERCOME THE CHALLENGE OF TOO MUCH

HANGING ON THE TELEPHONE

Frankly, these days the phone is more of a time saver than a time waster. Too many people send an email when a call would be both quicker and more effective at communicating your message.

The phone can, however, get in your way when:

You're on hold to a call centre. A headset or loudspeaker with the volume turned down can allow you to get on with low-level work while you are waiting. Or make use of the call back feature some call centres offer.

The phone interrupts you while you're working. Put your phone on silent if appropriate. But if you are interrupted, you have a short time to deal with it and not lose much of your recall of what you were working on. Use that time to test the caller: *'Is this something we can do in a minute or two? If it isn't, I'd like to give you my full attention, so when can I call you back?'* This way, you signal the call is important to you, while regaining control.

OVERCOME THE CHALLENGE OF TOO MUCH

DISTRACTIONS

1. **Interruptions**
   Unwelcome interruptions distract you from what you want to do, with something you don't.

   Of course, unwelcome doesn't mean you shouldn't deal with it. It may be urgent and important. Or you may be a manager, and helping your team member is your job.

2. **Procrastination**
   Enticing alternatives that distract you from what you know you should do, with something more appealing. When you succumb, this is called procrastination.

   Not all procrastination is bad. Sometimes we take the opportunity to do something important and the outcome is worthwhile. The thing you put off could wait, so there's no long-term problem.

OVERCOME THE CHALLENGE OF TOO MUCH

UNWANTED INTERRUPTIONS

Let me just…
When you get an interruption, get in the habit of saying *'let me just…'* to give you a few moments to save your work, put away confidential papers, get to a suitable break point, or make a note of what's in your mind to do next.

Allocated time
Do you allocate your work into time slots as advocated in Section 1? (see page 23) If you do, you can look the interrupter in the eye and say *'I'd love to. But I have something on. Can I get back to you at 3 o'clock?'*

Assertive NO
Or you could use your **N**oble **O**bjection (see page 64) to decline a request, and quickly get back to what you are doing.

OVERCOME THE CHALLENGE OF TOO MUCH

PREVENTING INTERRUPTIONS

There are two good ways to deflect interruptions before they get to you.

Signalling
If you can, establish a signal with the people around you, that makes it clear whether you are working on lightweight stuff and open to interruptions, or you are immersed in something important and don't want to be interrupted.

Some people use the angle of their chair, headphones, or a red/green traffic light system. I used to have a sign that said *'It's okay to interrupt me'*. Once, a colleague told me my sign had fallen over. *'No,'* I said, *'I turned it over.'* She never interrupted me again. The gold standard is an open or closed door, but who still has offices?

Escape
Ignore the last comment. The gold standard is really not being there to be interrupted. Find a meeting room to work in. Or, if it's appropriate, take your work to a café. If they can't find you, they can't... hang on; my phone's ringing.

BEAT PROCRASTINATION

How much time do you fritter away, doing nothing very much? It's easier than doing something important, which takes concentration and involves the possibility of failure. So you replace meaningful activity with meaningless *'displacement'* activities. This is procrastination; putting off what you know you need to do.

Remove distractions
How do you choose something other than what you should be doing? That's right, you get distracted: by a website, an email, social media, a magazine. Banish them.

Procrastination is comfortable
So remove the cosy feeling by focusing on what will go wrong if you continue to avoid what matters.

Work in small chunks
Don't try and do the whole job at once. Divide it up and give yourself a break between each chunk.

BEAT PROCRASTINATION

Start small
Start with a small part of the task. It need only be finding the relevant file or email. This is easy, so it won't disrupt the cosiness. Once past your initial reluctance to begin, momentum will kick in and you'll find yourself doing more than you intended.

Create pressure
It's easy to procrastinate when there are no consequences. Make a promise to someone, which you know you have to keep.

Choose your moment
Do you work best with a coffee, or first thing in the morning, or at the end of the day, or in a café? Know your preference and use it to tackle unwelcome tasks.

Celebrate success
Each time you complete a chunk, make a point of congratulating and rewarding yourself. Nothing motivates us like success.

We'll also meet two more ideas in the next section: frogs and tomatoes.

EVERYONE HAS A SYSTEM

LEARN FROM THE BEST

If you talk to enough people about how they manage their time you will find that everyone has a system of their own. These range from simple list-keeping, to elaborate frameworks.

In this section, we will survey eight of the most common systems. Each one is good at helping with one particular aspect of time management. Maybe one of them will help you.

- Eating Frogs
- Italian Tomatoes
- Getting Things Done®
- Setting Focus
- Urgent and Important
- Chain of Success
- Kanban
- Software Tools

Further references for all these systems can be found on page 111.

EATING FROGS

'Mark Twain once said that if the first thing you do each morning is to eat a live frog, you can go through the day with the satisfaction of knowing that that is probably the worst thing that is going to happen to you all day long.'

This is the hook to Brian Tracy's 2001 book *'Eat that Frog!'*, although, like so many quotes that are accredited to Twain, there is no evidence that he ever said it. The principle tracks back to 1790s France, where Nicolas Chamfort credited it to M. de Lassay. Back then, it was a toad, not a frog:

'Swallow a toad every morning, in order to fortify ourselves against the disgust of the rest of the day.'

Either way, the principle is simple: the frog represents the things you need to do but don't want to do. You aren't motivated to do them, so you procrastinate and they remain undone. The habit of eating a frog first thing makes you productive and avoids the rest of your day being dominated by the thing you are trying to avoid. And usually your willpower is at its greatest early in the day.

EATING FROGS

In his book, Tracy sets out a number of principles for eating frogs.

1. Identify all the things you want to do.

2. Start your day by eating the frog.

3. If you have two frogs to eat, start with the biggest, ugliest one.

4. The longer you look at it, the worse it gets.

5. Tuck in and work steadily through the frog, until it's all eaten.

6. Become addicted to getting a frog eaten each day, as your habit builds.

This is a brilliant procrastination beater; especially for when you know it must get done. It's the opposite of starting small. In my experience, it works best with a simple reward, to celebrate successfully swallowing something unpalatable.

EVERYONE HAS A SYSTEM

ITALIAN TOMATOES

'The Pomodoro Technique' takes its name from an Italian tomato. The author of the book, Francesco Cirillo, used a tomato-shaped kitchen timer as a student and now markets his own Pomodoro timers.

The principle is simple: time-boxing, or setting aside a fixed time to work on a single specific task. In the case of Pomodoro, the timer is set to 25 minutes. During that time, you don't accept any interruptions. At the end, an alarm rings.

As with Tracy's *'Eat that Frog'*, Pomodoro starts with a list of tasks. You then estimate how many Pomodoros (25 minute sprints) it will take to complete each. Between each Pomodoro, you take a short break. After four intervals, take a longer break.

The technique works for two main reasons:

1. 25 minutes is about the right time to maintain high energy focus.

2. It also reduces distractions and so maintains productive state.

85

ITALIAN TOMATOES

Here is a formulation of the Pomodoro process:

1. Select a task you need to focus on, from your list.

2. Set your timer to 25 minutes.

3. Work steadily with no distractions, and stop when the timer rings.

4. Mark off what you've achieved and review what you've learned.

5. Take a short (3-5 minute) break. Get up and move about.

6. Repeat three more times.

7. Take a longer break (20-30 minutes) after the fourth interval.

8. And repeat through the day.

This works best when you have a lot of smaller tasks, as it precludes (and even prevents) the chance of getting deeply immersed into those productive 'flow states'. It's best for people who get bored easily and find it hard to concentrate for long bursts.

EVERYONE HAS A SYSTEM

GETTING THINGS DONE

David Allen's book, *'Getting Things Done'*, presents an intricate time management system. As a result, it is off-putting for some people. For others, it presents a transformative approach.

The core principles within his book are:

- Relieving stress and releasing mental capacity, by emptying your brain of all the things you want to do, and transferring them to an external system, which can equally be electronic or paper-based

- The approach is 'bottom-up' in the sense that it starts with all your ideas for things to do, and synthesizes them upwards to your medium term and then life-scale goals

- There is a deliberate and detailed workflow to follow, that makes it appealing to people who want a 'system' and are prepared to invest time in it. But it puts off those who find it adds too much overhead to their time management

EVERYONE HAS A SYSTEM

GETTING THINGS DONE

Getting Things Done® presents a five-step workflow:

1. **Capture: collect what has your attention**
   Capture all your big and small ideas for things to do on paper or digitally.

2. **Clarify: process what it means (8 options)**
   Is a task actionable? If not, put it into trash (1), a 'maybe' file (2), or file it for
   reference (3). If it is, will it take more than one step? If so, it's a project that needs a
   plan (4). If not, and you can do it in under 2 minutes, do it now (5). If you can,
   delegate it, and record it on a 'waiting for' list (6). For the rest, decide whether to
   schedule it (7), or put it on a to do list (8).

3. **Organise: put it where it belongs**
   Divide your to do list into categories like domestic, work, calls, etc.

4. **Reflect: review your lists frequently**
   Tidy them up, update them, plan your projects, and schedule tasks.

5. **Engage: just do it**
   Do the tasks from your lists and projects, based on where your focus is.

EVERYONE HAS A SYSTEM

SETTING YOUR FOCUS

If Getting Things Done® offers a system that's too structured for some people, Mark Forster's *'Autofocus'* system may not be structured enough.

This makes it ideal for small numbers of tasks, for people who are under little time pressure, or for people who feel overwhelmed by their task list. The system eschews prioritisation of tasks by importance, focusing on the psychology of resistance. It uses your intuitive feelings about *'what next?'* Implicitly, it assumes that what you put off is not really important.

It is motivating because, although it's technically an open-ended to do list, you focus only on one page of your task list at a time. As this page stops growing when it's full, your work diminishes the list you're focused on. Also, you only work on a topic for as long as you choose, thus encouraging you to make a start.

Mark Forster is a best-selling time management author, but he has only published his Autofocus system online.

SETTING YOUR FOCUS

Here's how to use Mark Forster's Autofocus system.

1. Keep a single list in a notebook, with 20-40 lines per page.
2. Scan the items on the first incomplete page, but don't take action.
3. Review the page slowly to find one that stands out for you.
4. Work on that item for as long as you want to.
5. Cross the item off the list. Re-enter it at the end of the list if you didn't finish it.
6. Continue with the same page and only move onto the next page when you complete a review of the page without any item standing out.
7. If no items on a page stand out, dismiss everything that is left, highlighting them for later review.
8. Move onto the next page and repeat the process.
9. When you've finished with the last page, go back to the first page that still has active items.

EVERYONE HAS A SYSTEM

URGENT & IMPORTANT

'Most things which are urgent are not important, and most things which are important are not urgent.' Attributed to President Dwight D. Eisenhower

Stephen Covey took this simple truth and used it as the basis for one of his *'7 Habits of Highly Effective People'*, in his best-selling book of that name.

The formulation generates a two-by-two grid. The four combinations each have their own characteristics; focusing on those that are important makes you more effective.

This is a valuable approach to prioritising your tasks, and the quadrant where you get most control is *'Important but Not Urgent'*. It's there that you get stuff done before it becomes urgent. Thus your stress levels are low, and you have time to focus on what matters most in the long and short term.

URGENT & IMPORTANT

The four quadrants are:

Urgent and important tasks
These grab your attention and take top priority. They can feel like crises and, as they build up, you start to feel stressed and overwhelmed.

Not urgent but important tasks
Investment, preparation, and deliberate work that is productive and effective. Get things done here, before they become stress-inducing urgent and important tasks.

Urgent but not important tasks
Distractions and interruptions that leave you busy but unproductive. Often they represent others' short term priorities. Your response should be a **N**oble **O**bjection.

Not urgent and not important tasks
Trivia and displacement activities with little or no value. They waste your time and so cause procrastination. Eat a frog instead.

A CHAIN OF SUCCESS

This technique was reportedly described by comedian Jerry Seinfeld to web developer and stand-up comedian, Brad Isaac.

It's a technique for motivating you to persevere with an ongoing task, create a new habit, or work towards a big goal. Seinfeld used it to motivate himself to find time to write new material every day.

It's astonishingly simple and needs no technology (although yes, you can get an app). All you do is mark a big X on a calendar for every day that you do the thing you want to do. The rule is: *'don't break the chain.'*

It works because it creates a habit by motivating you to want to write your big X. And that's motivating because of both the visual dominance of that X, and the tactile pleasure of writing it. I suspect an app delivers less on both of these.

EVERYONE HAS A SYSTEM

A CHAIN OF SUCCESS

Here's how to create your own chain of success.

1. Decide on your goal (or goals – not too many).

2. Decide how much work to put in each day – and maybe the time of day you'll do it.

3. Put up a calendar in a prominent place.

4. Each day you complete your task, draw a big red X across that day on your calendar.

5. Don't break the chain.

What if you have to miss a day?
...for holidays or sickness, for perhaps.

You don't want to break the chain, but it's not your fault. How about allowing yourself a blue X, or a tick?

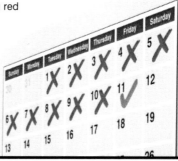

(94)

KANBAN

Kanban started life as an inventory control system at Toyota in the 1950s. It was developed by Taiichi Ohno as part of the Toyota Production System, supporting the idea of *'Just in Time'* manufacturing. The word means billboard.

It became popular as a time management tool when IT-based project managers adopted the Kanban Board to visualise progress on their projects. Each task is recorded on a card, which moves from one bin to another on a prominently visible Kanban Board. The names of the people responsible are also recorded on the cards.

In time management, Kanban is ideal for tracking the progress of tasks that need to go through a series of stages.

95

EVERYONE HAS A SYSTEM

KANBAN

Here's how to use a Kanban process for personal time management.

1. Determine the stages that make sense to you and draw up your Kanban Board.

2. Put each task that you could do onto a card with any information that's useful. You can also use coloured cards to code for different types of work.

3. As you start doing a task, move it to the next stage.

4. The board lets you see where each task is in the process, and what to work on next.

5. Sort cards by deadline or logical sequence, with higher priority cards at the top.

6. Keep the amount of 'work in progress' (WIP) at a level that suits you. This means having a maximum number of cards in the stages between 'could do' and 'done'.

SOFTWARE

Whether you prefer to use your phone, a tablet, or your computer, there are plenty of software tools available.

Most are now web-based and hosted in the cloud. This means you can easily synchronise your information between multiple devices. In our 'always on' world, you need never be apart from your time management software.

There are, of course, different types of tool, from the simplest list to the most complex tools, able to handle substantial projects. Also, many of the systems we've seen in this chapter have their own tools – some proprietary, others with numerous versions.

You will find tools for calendars, task lists, note-taking, reminders, email inbox management, time tracking, filing, Pomodoro, Getting Things Done®, Chain of Success, Kanban, goal-setting, personal accountability, and more.

97

EVERYONE HAS A SYSTEM

SOFTWARE

I'm not going to recommend any particular tool. Your preference is likely to be personal and new options appear almost daily. The technique is to:

1. Decide what type of tool you want to test out, eg Kanban, to do list, motivation.

2. Make a list of the features you really want, eg sorting, sharing, cloud-based.

3. Hit the search engine and find two or three tools that have those features.

4. Download trial versions or set up free accounts.

5. Try them out for yourself.

6. Settle on the one you find most easy to use and stick with it.

STRATEGIC TIME MANAGEMENT

STRATEGIC TIME MANAGEMENT

TIME IS MORE VALUABLE THAN ANY RESOURCE

It's a commonplace claim that *'people are our most valuable asset'*. But the truth is that people move on and are replaced. What you can never replace is time. Once it's gone, it's gone for good.

It is people's time that is an organisation's most valuable asset, yet it appears on no balance sheets. How would it be if an annual report had to include a balance sheet of how many working hours the organisation had to deploy at the start of the year, and how much it achieved with those hours? And how many it has going into the next year, and how it plans to spend them?

In a world where cycle times on innovation, product maturity, and company survival have diminished, we need to start treating time as the strategic asset it is. This means recognising we have the choice to determine:

- How much time we buy (number of people) and stop seeing it only as a cost

- How to deploy the time we have, for the greatest return

STRATEGIC TIME MANAGEMENT

A BIGGER JOB DOES NOT MEAN A BIGGER CLOCK

The most senior people in an organisation do not have more time than anyone else.

They may choose to give more of it to their work, but when work-life balance becomes a significant work-rest imbalance, that's just false accounting.

It's the most senior people who:

- Design their organisation's future

- Drive the changes that grow their business

- Develop the talent (asset base) of tomorrow

- Cultivate transformative relationships

Yet, too often, we hear of 'de-layering' and 'widening spans of control'. The effect of these is to load more and more onto people who have a fixed capacity. So they become bottlenecks in decision-making, and run from one crisis to another, never fully resolving anything. Familiar?

EXECUTIVE BUSYNESS

Two executives each oversee one product category. When one leaves, the corporation decides to save money and promote the remaining exec. So now, she has two categories to oversee. It sounds efficient. More recognition of talent, and cost savings to the business.

But pretty soon, she's getting overworked and stressed. Her day is a rush from one meeting to another. She doesn't have time to read her briefing notes, much less to think strategically. One-to-ones are rushed and morale drops. Work is delayed on key projects because she's not been able to get an update and make a decision. She's getting further behind, and more of her week is spent in crisis management. She's tired, finding it hard to shake a persistent cough, and her partner and children hardly see her.

This is not productivity. Nor is it effective. It's just busyness. And it's not sustainable. She needs to stop and rethink what matters in her new role, and how to deliver it.

STRATEGIC TIME MANAGEMENT

INITIATIVE OVERLOAD

Why do so many organisational projects fail?

Is it because project staff are lazy or incompetent? Are project processes inadequate? Is there a failure of estimation, or have stakeholders been inadequately consulted? Are they just bad at doing projects?

Of course some or all are true in certain cases. But a big reason for project failure has nothing to do with **how** organisations do projects. It is about **which** projects the organisation chooses to do. Or to be more precise; **how many** projects it does.

Project A is great. It will make money, save costs, and we have the skills to do it.

Project B is great too, for the same reasons.

So you should do both...
No. Not if you don't have the resources to deliver both. Strategic time management must include selecting the projects that deliver greatest net strategic benefit, and being prepared to cancel or defer others.

INVESTMENT IN RESOURCES

If you are a property management business, would you expect to make more money if you shed assets? Of course not. Assets – well-chosen – make a return.

So it is with the people in your business. Strategic time management means looking at people's time as an asset. Two managers can do twice as much as one. So they can deliver more strategic benefit.

A manager supported by a skilled executive assistant can do more than one working alone, planning their own travel and arranging their own meetings.

Investing in this way pays off double. You create an environment where people know they can do their best work. For many of us, this is a source of pride and intrinsic motivation. It helps with overall productivity and with retention.

In the race to the bottom of the pond, however, you may not win. But you will find yourself swimming in the muck that circulates there.

LEADERSHIP LEVERAGE

A good leader can achieve tasks well beyond their personal capacity, by leverage: deploying the capabilities of their team.

Well-honed leadership skills, supported by the right infrastructure, can achieve near infinite leverage. One person can lead a giant corporation, a vast army, or a whole nation. But leadership time is not, and can never be infinite.

Indeed, a leader has no more time in their day than anyone else. So, the choice an organisation must make is either to boost the leadership leverage or reduce its leaders' workload.

Realistically, most leadership teams are unable to recruit substantial extra resources. So, if the leaders are to achieve more with what they have, they must be more selective about what they choose to drop.

STRATEGIC RESPONSIBILITIES

People in a managerial role may work 220 days a year, or 55 days per quarter. In that time, they need to:

- Manage the day-to-day business within their area of responsibility
- Grow, improve and transform that business
- Manage people and relationships
- Carry out their own administrative tasks

If that's you, what proportion of your time does each of these merit? Think about the strategic value each can deliver. Also think about the risk attached to each: what are the consequences of failures, and how likely are they?

Now look at your diary for the last two or three weeks. How well does your reality match your priorities?

You can go a step further. Draw up a quarterly time budget for yourself – as on the next page.

TIME BUDGET

For your budget, identify five crucial priorities for the quarter. Allocate 95 percent of your time (50-55 days, typically) to them, retaining 5 percent for necessary admin. Then determine your essential outcomes for those priorities and check you can reasonably achieve them in the days you have allotted. If you have people working for you, assign one or more of your priorities to each of them. Help them split their time among more detailed priorities and determine the outcomes from that time. Now everyone in your team is working to the same set of strategic priorities.

Strategic Time Budget   Period

Priority 1	Priority 2	Priority 3
• Outcome	• Outcome	• Outcome
• Outcome	• Outcome	• Outcome
• Outcome	• Outcome	• Outcome
Total days:	Total days:	Total days:

ORGANISATIONAL TIME

Let's see how your organisation can systematically make better use of its time.

Better meetings
Cancel meetings you don't need, shorten meetings you do, and only invite people that really need to be there. Tighten agendas and enforce preparation discipline.

Encourage breaks
Reset expectations and make proper breaks the norm.

Work management tools
Invest in organisation-wide software that helps people use their time effectively.

Micro-goals
Remember Amabile and Kramer's research? (See page 15). Break big outcomes into frequent milestones to keep motivation levels high.

Training and workshops
Deliver training and workshops that let people share tips and explore bottlenecks.

THE GIFT OF TIME

In his book, *'Give and Take'*, Adam Grant spells out one of the strongest predictors of group effectiveness. It's when people help each other.

Collaboration is another example of spending time to create better productivity. The people he refers to as *'givers'* give their time to coach, train, advise and share knowledge with others. When others reciprocate, everyone wins.

The idea of competition and pitting colleagues against one another sounds like it will get the best from everyone, but in truth only a few will thrive. In a culture of reciprocal giving, everyone can thrive. You need to weed out those Grant calls 'takers'.

But the givers need time to work on their own stuff, so you must first ensure that they can set aside quiet times and have access to quiet spaces, so their inclination to give does not overwhelm their need to deliver. And second, you must encourage everyone to ask for help when they need it.

THE NATURE OF TIME

Life deals us the hand we need to play. Modern life seems to deal off a thousand decks and gives us a hand with ever more cards. If you are like all the managers, leaders, and professionals I meet, you constantly have too much to do.

So working life, family life, and your social life are all a stream of choices. You can only play one card at a time. Which one?

That's why I'm no fan of systems. Instead, I prefer broad principles, and a well-stocked box of tools to apply to different situations. To me, a system is a principle applied rigidly. And at some point, it won't apply. That's why I filled this Pocketbook with ideas to try; not just a single system.

As a young man, I studied physics. If anyone tells you that you can manage time; they're lying. Nobody even understands time. But what we do know, is that tomorrow 24 hours will have gone. Forever.

So treat time as the precious strategic asset that it is. Or waste it like disposable packaging. It's your choice.